LET'S LEARN ABOUT SPACE

COMETS

Rebecca Kraft Rector

Enslow Publishing
101 W. 23rd Street
Suite 240
New York, NY 10011
USA

enslow.com

Words to Know

coma The gas cloud around the nucleus of a comet.

diameter How wide an object is.

head The coma and nucleus of a comet.

nucleus The solid core of a comet.

orbit The path of an object as it circles another object in space.

oval Shaped like an egg.

solar system The sun and the bodies that move around it.

tail The dust and gas that stream from a comet.

CONTENTS

A comet looks like a bright streak in the night sky.

What Is a Comet?

A comet is a chunk of ice, gas, and dust. Comets are in outer space. Comets **orbit** the sun. About 100,000 million comets orbit the sun.

FAST FACT
Comets are called "dirty snowballs."

A spacecraft explores the outer solar system. This is where most comets from.

Where Do Comets Come From?

Long ago, planets formed. Pieces were left over. Some became comets. There are billions of comets. Most comets come from the outer solar system.

Comets make an oval as they go around the sun.

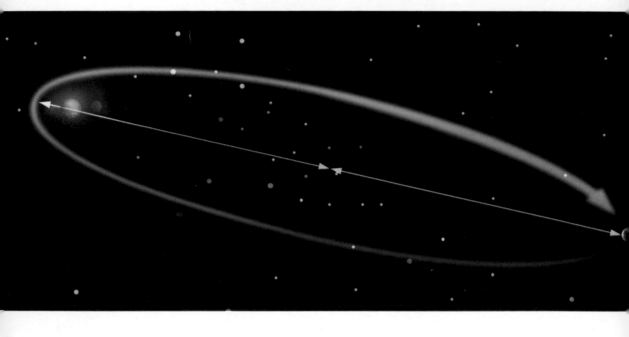

Long and Short Orbits

Comets have an **oval** orbit. Some orbits are long. Thousands of years pass as the comets travel. Some orbits are short. They last only a few years.

FAST FACT
Comets orbit near the sun, then far away.

The main body of the comet is the nucleus. The one you see here is more than a mile long.

The Nucleus

The comet's **nucleus** is a chunk of ice. It is the solid part of the comet. It holds ice, dust, and frozen gases. The nucleus is often several miles across.

FAST FACT
The nucleus is usually a dark color.

The gas and dust
around the nucleus of
the comet is the coma.

The Coma

Comets warm up when they go near the sun. Some of the ice changes to gas. The gas surrounds the nucleus. This cloud of gas is called the **coma**.

FAST FACT

The coma can be a million miles (1.6 million kilometers) in diameter.

Together, the coma and the nucleus make up the comet's head.

The Head

The nucleus and coma are called the head. The gas cloud makes the head look fuzzy. The comet cools away from the sun. The coma disappears. Only the nucleus is left.

FAST FACT
The head of a comet is usually larger than Earth.

A comet's long, bright tail can make it easy to spot.

The Tail

The sun's energy pushes the coma away. A yellow dust **tail** forms. A blue gas tail also forms. The tail can be millions of miles long.

FAST FACT

The comet's tail points away from the sun.

**This picture of Halley's Comet
is part of a tapestry that is
almost a thousand years old.**

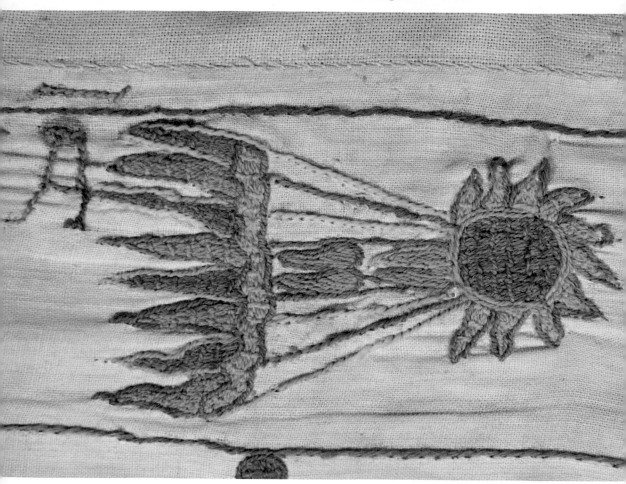

Seeing Comets

Sometimes comets can be seen from Earth. People saw them long ago. They made pictures of them. They called them long-haired stars.

FAST FACT

Halley's Comet can be seen every 76 years.

A spacecraft (at the bottom of the photo) landed on this comet in 2014.

Studying Comets

Scientists study comets. Computers and cameras help find comets. Spacecraft send back information. This helps us learn how the solar system formed.

Activity

Catch That Comet!

Make your own comet. Watch it fly through space!

MATERIALS

plastic bag
tennis ball
scissors
string or ribbon

Procedure:

Step 1: Put the ball in the bag.

Step 2: Tie the bag close to the ball.

Step 3: Cut the plastic into strips below the ball.

Step 4: Tie long ribbons below the ball.

Toss your comet. The tennis ball is the nucleus. The bag is the coma. The tails stream behind.

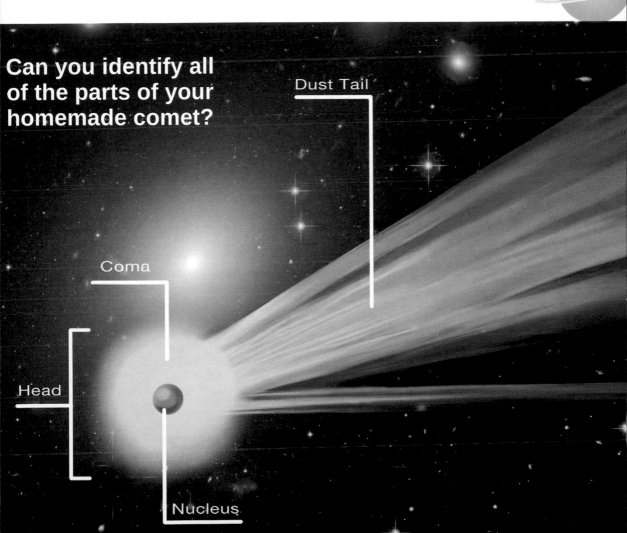

Can you identify all of the parts of your homemade comet?

Dust Tail

Coma

Head

Nucleus

LEARN MORE

Books

Hansen, Grace. *Comets.* Minneapolis, MN: Abdo Kids, 2018.

Riggs, Kate. *Comets.* Mankato, MN: Creative Education, 2015.

Stiefel, Chana. *Comets and Meteors.* Vero Beach, FL: Rourke Educational Media, 2015.

Websites

NASA—Comet Quest
spaceplace.nasa.gov / comet-quest / en /
Explore a comet in this fun game.

NASA—Comets
starchild.gsfc.nasa.gov / docs / StarChild / solar_system_level1 / comets.html
Check out facts about comets.

Science Kids—Comet Facts for Kids
www.sciencekids.co.nz / sciencefacts / space / comets.html
Enjoy fun comet facts.

INDEX

Published in 2020 by Enslow Publishing, LLC.
101 W. 23rd Street, Suite 240, New York, NY 10011

Copyright © 2020 by Enslow Publishing, LLC.

Library of Congress Cataloging-in-Publication Data

Names: Rector, Rebecca Kraft, author.
Title: Comets / Rebecca Kraft Rector.
Description: New York : Enslow Publishing, 2020. | Series: Let's learn about space | Audience: Grade K to 4. | Includes bibliographical references and index.
Identifiers: LCCN 2018041864| ISBN 9781978507272 (library bound) | ISBN 9781978509221 (pbk.) | ISBN 9781978509238 (6 pack)
Subjects: LCSH: Comets—Juvenile literature.
Classification: LCC QB721.5 .R43 2019 | DDC 523.6—dc23

LC record available at https://lccn.loc.gov/2018041864

Printed in the United States of America

To Our Readers: We have done our best to make sure all website addresses in this book were active and appropriate when we went to press. However, the author and the publisher have no control over and assume no liability for the material available on those websites or on any websites they may link to. Any comments or suggestions can be sent by e-mail to customerservice@enslow.com.

Photo Credits: Cover, p. 1 solarseven/Shutterstock.com; p. 4 NASA/JPL-Caltech/UCLA; p. 6 Mark Garlick/Science Photo Library/Getty Images; p. 8 BSIP/Science Source; p. 10 NASA/JPL-Caltech/UMD; p. 12 NASA/SSPL/Getty Images; p. 14 Visuals Unlimited, Inc./Alan Dyer/Getty Images; p. 16 Alan Dyer/Stocktrek Images/Getty Images; p. 18 Walter Rawlings/robertharding/Getty Images; p. 20 ESA/Rosetta/Philae/CIVA via NASA; p. 23 Spencer Sutton/Science Source/Getty Images; interior design elements (planets) Vectomart/Shutterstock.com, (sun) Kirill Kirsanov/Shutterstock.com.